Splitting Souls

Briar T Quinn

BookLeaf Publishing

India | USA | UK

Presentation by *BookLeaf Publishing*

Web: www.bookleafpub.com

E-mail: info@bookleafpub.com

ISBN: 9789357445733

First edition 2022

ACKNOWLEDGEMENT

Thank you to Neil Hilborn, without whose writing workshops I wouldn't have had the courage to begin poetry again.

On a Thread

It was only a matter of time before we snapped
You had me on a string I thought came from
your heart
But was instead just wound around your finger
And I clung to it like a lifeline, a fish caught on
a hook
Struggling and gasping in the air but goddamn if
the sun didn't look so beautiful out of that water

You choked me, gutted me, flayed me open wide
And I let you put those ropes around my wrists
to hold me down
Hold me back
Hold me right inside your arms where I was
captive, captivated
Isn't this just the way you wanted me, baby?

Tossed out in the dirt when you were done
Bored of your game, knot got frayed, string
coming loose
Me, coming undone, you, unbothered by what
you had done
The string was floss, the floss is frail, I am
falling by the wayside

And you are driving into that starry sky
Unharmed
And I will never be unmarked

Alaska

Blue like the way melancholy songs breathe
through my heart
Blue like bipolar nebulas, or butterfly nebulas,
or two full moons in a month
Like the color of morning glories, dew dripping
from the petals in the morning
Like the way rain tastes in summer
Blue like thunder rolling across the sky,
ominous, calming

Blue like the color of the eyes in every country
love song
Like waking up pre-dawn and hearing the
softness of the earth
Blue like Seattle
Blue like Chicago
Like the color of the drugs in my treasure chest,
my lifeline
Like dipping your toes in a river and watching
the way the water moves
Blue like the birds who throw themselves at my
kitchen window

Blue like violence

Blue, the color my fingers turn in winter because
I always forget my gloves
Like the way sweet tea tastes in the summer heat
Like love gone wrong
Like the bruises on my wrists
Blue like the feeling when I escaped

But green like the color of fresh grass
Like the color of spring and new beginnings
Like the specks in the eyes of my new forever
love
Green like the mint of the tie he wore on our
wedding day
Green like Seattle
Green like two trees, intertwining at last,
growing together
Like they were always reaching for each other
Like they finally found home

Little Bird

I wish I had been born a bird, like so many
people say I am
Safe inside a small, hard shell until I chose to
come out
Then protected by my mother's wings when
danger was near
Taken care of diligently until I was ready to be
on my own
I desperately wish I had been born a bird

Birds still self-harm, in a way
Feather-picking and self-mutilating
For much the same reasons as humans
Loneliness, trauma, stress
And I know that if I were to be a bird
With the same mother as I have as a human
I would pick my feathers until I could no longer
fly

I was never meant to be my mother's child
Too much for her to handle; too sick, too sad,
*too old to be crying this much you need to grow
up*
Pushed from the nest far too soon

I could not hold my weight in the sky, only hop
along the ground and hope for the best
And from below I watched the newest egg hatch,
coddled, loved, and prized
And I wondered what I could have done
differently

They say even caged birds sing but I was never
given a voice
So as I lie upon the ground surrounded by my
torn out feathers
I cannot even cry out for the mother who never
loved me
Just weep for the sky I never got to reach

Addiction

The kitchen knife. The potato peeler. The small piece of broken glass on the window above the kitchen sink.
My mother tosses groceries on the counter and barks at me to put them away.
The ice cubes? Salt and ice.
Put away the potatoes.
The potato peeler.

Put away the apples, the milk, the frozen pizzas.
Salt and ice.
Sun seeps into the kitchen and I glance out the window.
The small piece of broken glass above the kitchen sink.
The kitchen knife.
The kitchen knife.
The kitchen knife.

False Psalms

God's feathers will protect you
Or so says Psalm 91:4
"With His feathers He will cover you"
A gentle shelter to ease your worries
And heal your tender heart

I need no feathers from God

I am my own small bird, colorful, strong
And I too, will protect you, but not with feathers
so weak
I fight with my claws out, beak sharp, voice
sharper
Wings beating out a windstorm no foe could
withstand

I am small, yes, but I am fierce and I am finding
my voice
My colors are more vivid than ever
And when you need a gentle sort of protection I
will sing, I will keep you safe beneath my
rainbow wings

Because tearing out my feathers to keep others
warm is not how I intend to live anymore

The Dead Still Speak

I have no skeletons in my closet
Only bodies beneath my bed
Skeletons equal regret and I have none left
But the bodies still speak
With rotting mouths and chewed up tongues
I've tried to dig graves for them but they always
find their way back
Making a home beneath my mattress
And whispering in the night

One tells me he had nothing but good intentions
The road to hell is paved with his blood
The handrails are his heartstrings, he says
He never meant any harm
And he clutches a diamond necklace in a tight
bony fist

One tells me she is the victim, here
Why am I casting her out so harshly, trying to
bury her love?

Her conditional, material, measuring tape around
my waist love
OCD turned PTSD and it all makes sense

The last is a girl, small
I don't try to bury her, but I do keep her in a
cozy box
She's got my baby blanket and stuffed bunny
and every comfort I can offer
But I can't let her out again
I know she'd look up to me, now

But I can't risk letting her ruin the progress I've
made

The Major's Soul

We are all just bags of emotions floating inside
hearts too small
And brains unequipped to process them
Once the emotions overtake us we begin to feel
them beyond our chests
Down, down to our toes, feel ghosts in our
navels
And when the ghosts take over, that's when the
panic sets in

I saw my fathers first panic attack seven years
after he saw mine
He didn't know what to do so I gave him a
Valium and called his doctor
My mother always told me we were too much
alike
One drunken night admitting that was the reason
she favored my sister
And in that moment I saw it so clear

My father is a strong man, too stubborn for
suicide
And I suppose I should thank him for that exact
trait

Because goddamnit, if I have to deal with me, so
does the rest of the world
We both wear battle scars for the world to see
And ones tucked away for family photos, big
smiles all around
We share the same laugh lines on our faces
And secret horrors behind our eyes

During bonfire nights I see his ghosts more
clearly
They drift from his navel and creep around and
up his spine
So I hug him close and remind him to look at the
beauty of the world
He'll kiss my head and call me a blessing and
I'll see the ghost retreat
And wish I could exorcise him of all his pain

I am my fathers child in every way, as long as
we steer clear of politics
We are a lifetime of quirks and trauma and
inside jokes bundled into a rucksack
But I do know this
One day his heart will cease to beat, and his
voice will no longer ring in my ear
One day I will only have dog tags and old
sweatshirts and an Army jacket or two
And the ghost of Jack Daniels on his breath

He will be returned to the universe as star dust,
and his soul will release all the happiness he's
gathered over the years back into this world
But parts of me will turn to dust too
And I just don't know how to make that poetic

Passing On

everything I learned from my mother
was simply
what not to do

I learned compassion from depression's
            fingertips
and how to love by inverting what I saw
            when my father was
                    gone

it's hard to unpack these musty boxes
but the dandelions are in bloom
and she always called them weeds
                while I called them wishes
so as I watch the wind carry them away
            I remember

    I am allowed to let this go, too

Putting it Down

My heart has always beat too fast—
Thumping in my chest like it doesn't belong
Pushing blood through my veins like it never
wants it back
At 13 I tried to give my heart it's wish
And instead collected the first scar upon my
wrist

I used to be ashamed of my scars;
Never wearing shorts in summer and keeping
my arms crossed
But now I wear them proudly
"Look how far I've come"
"See how much I've lived"
"I am still living"

Life dealt me a bullshit hand
A collection of mental illnesses and a little
autism to spice things up
I have a list of medications as long as the silence
I hear
After saying "I don't want to live anymore"
But even if I mean it in that moment
Don't believe it will last forever

Because despite all I have lived through in these
31 years
I never believed I'd make it to 31 in the first
place
And that is it's own small accomplishment
To live past the life expectancy you set for
yourself in your darkest days
How magical it is to live these days I could have
missed
How beautiful it is to see myself grow
And keep counting each day I make it through as
a trophy
A prize I never knew I was even reaching for

Still Frame

sometimes i wonder if looking up at the night
sky
still reminds you of me
the way we'd lean on the hood of your car and
wait for that slow shutter
this slow shudder
the way you'd brush your lips to mine under the
milky way
and grasp my hand in the cold night air

do you ever wonder if i am happy without you?
do you hope i am?
do you wonder if i still look at the stars and
think of you?
i sometimes do
i cling to those memories as the only good ones I
have of you left
and can't help but wish you nothing but regret

Midwest Ocean

Is the light at the end of the tunnel supposed to
be dim or bright?
Is the tunnel the symbolism or my life or my
depression?
Either way this tunnel is filling with water
I don't know how; I live in the middle of Iowa,
not on a beach or some shore
But I'm beginning to drown in it, I need help,
I'm sinking
I've forgotten how to swim and I have no life
jacket
This is not how I want to go
Let me go with the light in my hair, lying in a
bed of forget-me-nots
Or supine under the Milky Way—let the stars
take me
But not like this
I need more than one light
I need fewer tunnels and less water in my lungs
I need to feel the sun
I need to feel alive again

Heaven

The morning I got the call I had already written
my suicide note
It was tucked on my desk neatly beside my
favorite books
Waiting to be read by my mother, who would
surely find me first

The morning I got the call I showered and
dressed comfortably—just in case
In case it didn't work and I ended up in the
hospital again
In case it did and I ended up...somewhere,
forever, without a change of clothes

The morning I got the call I was ready

Then I got the call

And my world smashed to pieces like a sphere
of blown glass on cement

My father, unable to speak
My stepmom, taking the phone

"Your grandpa passed."

Thinking, I can't make my father lose his dad
and his daughter, too
Thinking, maybe this was a sign
Thinking, grandpa always told me to never give
up
Thinking, I gave up on God so long ago but
maybe he hadn't given up on me
Thinking, I have to burn that letter
Thinking, "this too shall pass"

The morning I got the call I had already written
my suicide note
After the call, I burned it and said thank you to a
God I didn't believe in

Semicolon

Hard comma, baby
We could never quite call it quits
We stop and go; stop and go
A mess of breakups and make-ups
You leave and I stay; I wait and you return

We were never meant for forever; we know
We've always known but we are pulled together
We can't escape the gravity of it
We can't escape the pull of the moon; the push
of the stars

This love was never love; lust, obsession,
possession, a game
No winners, just losers
Damned from the beginning but doomed to play
Five years of intertwining chain linked rusted
fences
Five years down a dirty drain

Perhaps it was destiny; cruel and eventual
Trapped together in an endless loop
We finally escaped one summer night
Said goodbye; never looked back

Managed to find the period we'd been searching
for
And finally called it quits.

Slashing Away

My mother's grasp
Too much to get away from
As hard as I tried
I was always spinning out of control
Her rein over me too strong; family first
Her controlling hand so tight
Her voice an echo in my head for too many
years
Tearing me apart no matter how hard I tried to
put myself together

Her baggage became my own
And it was so heavy to carry
A collection of diet pills, jeans too small,
resentment and spite
Passive aggressive text messages and
backhanded gifts

She told me I was weak
But I can wield my father's sword now
It may be too long but it feels light in my hand
I will fight with it as long as I can
And never let it go

Hermès Lead Us Home

The beautiful thing about human hearts and they
way they pump blood through our fragile bodies
Is the way they pump the intentions of our
futures within them too
Throbbing with the way things one day will be,
if only we let them

Soulmates are not what you would believe them
to be—no "one true love" or "happily ever after"
They are those who carry pieces of your heart
within them from their birth
Only to gently put them into place when you
finally meet; the kind of love that will never die

Aphrodite could be the goddess of soulmates but
an argument could be made for Dionysus
At least for you and me
All the madness of love and almost-love and
broken hearts driving us together like car crashes
in the night

Drinking wine coolers on Christmas evening and
taking comfort in just existing together

You are my hometown, after all, taking me
under your wing
This small wanderer who never really had a
home until she found your heart
And though we may lose our way when the
moon doesn't shine and the clouds cover the
stars
At least we'll walk this road together, avoiding
potholes and jumping in snow banks and
dancing in the rain

And Hermès will lead us home

Tip-Toe

You can't put a broken heart back together. Birds fly south for the winter to get free from the snow but I love the snow the way Midwest crops love the sun. Mermaids probably aren't real but if they are my best friend is doing a really good job hiding the fact that she is one. Autistic women don't get diagnosed at the same rate autistic men do. I walk on my toes and my friends call me a bird. The sky is too small to hold us all safely. Tolkien created the only world I feel safe in. If mermaids were real they'd be a queer-safe community. My first broken heart was when my dad left for Iraq. Hummingbird hearts flutter the way mine does during a panic attack. You can never quite fill a bowl with a crack in it, not even with sea water or sand. I want to fly away, like the bird they say I am.

Undercover

Who knew ptsd could be like cigarette smoke
You get that shit secondhand
Like gunshot wounds to the heart
Tear ducts at the ready
Numbness following like the ghost of who he
used to be
Iraq, Afghanistan, teenage me, he found God
again, over and over
It's getting so old
Like gunshot wounds to the heart
Emptying chambers into empty chambers
Helicopter blades like knives across my thighs
Scars the world can see, not the ones we share
We share so much but don't speak of it
Dirty little secrets like smoke bombs in the dead
of night
Waiting
Waiting
Waiting
Until finally the bomb drops
And we both explode like hand grenades

Panic

Five things to see
Your eyes, your lips, your shoulders broad; your
furrowed brow, your large hands holding mine

Four things to touch
Your skin, your fingertips, your palms, your
cheeks

Three things to hear
Your deep breaths, your deep voice, your deep
concern

Two things to smell
Your body; vanilla and musk. Your hair; apples
crisp and sharp

One thing to taste
Relief on my tongue; like Valium, like ice cold
water, like the way you bring me back to myself

Crash

Eleven pm and six degrees outside
Holding my hand while music played under the
street light
Freezing noses and colder fingers
But your smile warmed my heart

You called me a breeze on a warm day when I
called myself a tornado
And you have been my bomb shelter basement
through all these years
Dancing in the rain together
Snow angels and stargazing
Car crashes and panic filled lungs
Amethysts and meteorite rings

We met, then drifted
Met again and connected
And while I do not know where this life will
take us next
I know that our split souls came together that
summer night
And we were never meant to be parted again

www.ingramcontent.com/pod-product-compliance
Lightning Source LLC
Chambersburg PA
CBHW070724160726
48003CB00006BA/2365